MAMBO ITALIANO

Steve Galluccio

Talonbooks
2004

Talonbooks
P.O. Box 2076, Vancouver, British Columbia, Canada V6B 3S3
www.talonbooks.com

Typeset in New Baskerville and printed and bound in Canada.

First Printing: February 2004

National Library of Canada Cataloguing in Publication Data

Galluccio, Steve, 1960–
    Mambo italiano / Steve Galluccio.

A play.
ISBN 0-88922-494-3

    I. Title.
PS8563.A456M35 2004   C812'.6   C2003-907502-8

The publisher gratefully acknowledges the financial support of the
Canada Council for the Arts; the Government of Canada through the
Book Publishing Industry Development Program; and the Province of
British Columbia through the British Columbia Arts Council for our
publishing activities.

BRITISH
COLUMBIA
ARTS COUNCIL
Supported by the Province of British Columbia

Canadä

For my family

Mambo Italiano was first performed in French, translated by Michel Tremblay, at La Compagnie Jean-Duceppe, Montreal, Quebec, on December 13, 2000 with the following cast:

ANGELO . . . . Michel Poirier
ANNA . . . . Adèle Reindhardt
NINO . . . . Patrice Godin
PINA . . . . Maude Guérin
MARIA . . . . Véronique LeFlaguais
LINA . . . . Pierrette Robitaille
ANGELA . . . . Mireille Deyglun
GINO . . . . Normand Lévesque

Directed by Monique Duceppe
Set Design by Marcel Dauphinais
Props and Costume Design by Anne Duceppe
Lighting Design by Luc Prairie
Sound Design by Claude Lemelin
Stage Manager: Carol Gagné

The first English language production of *Mambo Italiano* was produced by Centaur Theatre Company, Montreal, Quebec, on September 27, 2001 with the following cast:

ANGELO . . . . Andreas Apergis
ANNA . . . . Ellen David
NINO . . . . Joseph Gallaccio
PINA . . . . Suzanna Le Nir
MARIA . . . . Mary Long
LINA . . . . Penny Mancuso
GINO . . . . Michel Perron

Directed by Gordon McCall
Set, Costume, and Props Design by John C. Dinning
Lighting Design by Luc Prairie
Stage Manager: Christina Hidalgo
Assistant Stage Manager: Merissa Tordjman
Assistant to the Director: Vania Rose

ACT ONE

Scene 1: Maria and Gino's House

*Set is dark. Loud music plays. Wash comes up on
Barbieri family. ANGELO, mid-thirties, MARIA, mid-
sixties, and GINO, mid-sixties. MARIA is visibly upset by
the ear-splitting music. Both MARIA and GINO speak
with Italian accents.*

MARIA

> (*shouting*) Could somebody please turn that music
> down!
>
> *Music continues to play.*
>
> (*shouting louder*) *Per favore!* Turn down the *musica!*
>
> *Music stops. ANNA, late thirties, enters with a bowl of
> salad, sets it on the table and sits down.*
>
> (*to ANNA*) I told you to turn it down, not to shut it off.

ANNA

> When you say "turn it down" it always means to shut it
> off.

GINO

> What's wrong with a little music while we're eating?

MARIA

> It was too loud, it was giving me a headache ... Anna
> go turn the music back on. I don't want your father
> accusing me of ruining his supper.

GINO

Never mind Anna. I don't want your mother to get one of her headaches because of my music.

ANNA

(*upset*) But it was *my* music!

ANGELO

(*to change the subject*) Your lasagna is really good, *mamma*.

MARIA

(*affectionately*) *Grazie* Angelo.

(*not so affectionate*) But it's not good enough to keep you living at home, ah?

ANNA

If there's gonna be another argument about why Angelo isn't living here anymore, I'm leaving the table!

GINO

No one leaves this table until supper is over!

ANNA pours herself some wine. MARIA stops her.

MARIA

One glass of wine is enough!

ANNA

It's my first glass!

MARIA

It's your second!

GINO

If your mother says it's your second, it's your second!

ANGELO

(*sarcastic*) There's nothing like a relaxing evening at home!

MARIA
Why is this not relaxing? What are your ignorant Italian parents doing wrong now?

ANGELO
It was just a joke, ma.

MARIA
Save your stupid jokes for your plays.

GINO
(*to ANGELO*) Angelo, your cousin Franca just got a promotion at work. She says if you want her old job, it's yours. Call her Monday.

ANGELO
Pa, I have a job.

MARIA
You don't have a job.

ANNA
But *mamma*, he's a writer!

GINO
That should be his hobby!

ANGELO
Hobby? Pa, I write for a sitcom. I've won awards. My plays have been produced all over. I'm published!

MARIA
But where's the security in that, ah?

GINO
Where's the pension plan, ah?

ANGELO
(*exasperated*) But ... I ... Anna, you talk to them.

ANNA

(*to ANGELO*) This is the part where you pour yourself another glass of wine.

ANGELO

(*to MARIA and GINO*) Then you guys wonder why I left?

MARIA

Si, we wonder. What is so wrong with living at home until you get married? Both your father and me did it, and we're not dead.

GINO

We're still here.

MARIA

And after we got married we had both our mothers living with us.

GINO

And your crazy Aunt Yolanda, until she got married.

MARIA

(*shouting*) My sister Yolanda was not crazy!

ANNA

She was so cool. She'd always put the radio on full blast and dance around the apartment.

ANGELO

But didn't you guys ever wanna be out on your own?

MARIA

What for? What's so special about being out on my own?

GINO

Nothing at all!

MARIA

Besides, you're not on your own. You got a roommate.

ANGELO

It's less expensive that way, ma.

GINO

If you were still living with us, it would cost you nothing at all!

MARIA

Why you prefer living with a perfect stranger than with me and your father and your sister, I don't know.

ANGELO

Stranger? I live with Nino, ma. *Nino!* We've known each other since we were kids. You were friends with his parents back in Italy.

MARIA

But do we really know *him*?

GINO

We don't him at all.

ANGELO

I know him! That's what's important!

MARIA

Always thinking of yourself! ... Excuse us for trying to understand *why* you would rather live with Nino, than with your own flesh and blood.

GINO

Who would rather die, than let anything happen to you.

MARIA

Why is he a better roommate than us, ah?

GINO

Why?

ANGELO

Because!

MARIA & GINO
    Because why?

        Beat.

ANGELO
    (*shouting*) Because Nino's my lover!

        *GINO, MARIA, and ANNA freeze. ANGELO addresses the
        audience.*

Now if I could only say that out loud. "Nino's my
lover!"

        *ANGELO gets up from the dinner table as the wash fades
        on his family.*

But I can't. Every time I try to, I freeze. No one knows
I'm gay. Except for my sister. And I don't know how
much longer I can keep this up. And the worst thing
about it, is that my mother keeps on setting me up with
all these "nice Italian girls." And like an idiot I go out
on these dates. Then I have to make up some story of
why "the girl was not for me." Well, no more! No more!
… Yeah right Angelo, no more … I'm telling you,
being gay and Italian is a fate worse than … actually,
there is no fate worse than being gay and Italian …

        *Wash crossfades to Angelo's apartment. The apartment's
        decor is modern, tasteful, and gives the allure of being
        inhabited by people who have done well. NINO,
        mid-thirties, is sitting on the couch watching television.
        ANGELO still addresses the audience.*

There he is. My Nino. Just as gorgeous as the first time
I *really* noticed him. It was at a basketball game back in
high school. Not that I liked basketball, I just enjoyed
looking at sweaty almost-naked guys bouncing their
balls around … anyway … *there* was Nino. King of the
basketball team. And next thing I know, nothing else

mattered, except for Nino. And everything went dark, except for Nino … He ignored me throughout high school. We went to different universities. I lost complete sight of him. Until one day I needed an accountant, and I went to this firm, and I was waiting in an office, and in walks Nino. King of the firm. So he did my taxes, one thing led to another as they say, and before long, he moved in with *me*. (*approaches NINO*) We've been together for about a year now, and still, every time I look at him, nothing else matters. Except for Nino. And everything goes dark. Except for Nino.

> *ANGELO walks over to the apartment. Scene 2 begins.*

Scene 2: Angelo and Nino's Apartment

> *ANGELO stands behind NINO. NINO grabs his arms. Caresses them. The two roughhouse a bit. ANGELO playfully pushes him away. Loud dance music is heard. Then fades. Then gets louder. Crowds are heard cheering. The music and the crowd noises (going loud and soft) will be heard throughout the scene.*

ANGELO
What are you watching?

NINO
The soccer match, but with all the racket that's going on outside, (*gets up, upset*) it's pretty hard to follow.

(*shouting, as if out of a window*) Shut up!

> *ANGELO joins NINO near the window (which faces the audience).*

ANGELO
Oh no … is it that time of year again?

NINO
    Yes. (*with disdain*) Gay pride.

ANGELO
    Close the window.

NINO
    It's too damn hot. Next year we're moving. I don't
    wanna have to deal with these idiots anymore.

ANGELO
    (*with disgust*) Look at them. Parading down the street
    half-naked. Drag queens, drag kings, transvestites.

NINO
    Fags!

            ANGELO and NINO tongue-kiss.

ANGELO
    (*smelling his neck*) Is that the aftershave I gave you?

NINO
    Uh-huh.

ANGELO
    Sexy.

            ANGELO and NINO kiss again. Cheering grows louder.

NINO & ANGELO
    Shut up!

NINO
    They even have the balls to wave at the TV cameras!
    What are their parents gonna think?

ANGELO
    Did you ever wonder what it might be like to be out of
    the closet?

NINO

No … (*cuddles with ANGELO*) … it's so warm and comfy in here.

> *ANGELO and NINO kiss.*

ANGELO

Did you ever feel like telling anyone?

NINO

Your sister knows, that's more than enough. Don't tell me you wanna come out on me.

ANGELO

No way.

> *Beat. They kiss again.*

Although I think my parents might suspect.

NINO

What's to suspect? We both have our own bedrooms …

ANGELO

And we're macho studs!

NINO

Oh yeah!

> *NINO grabs ANGELO, pulls him towards him and they kiss. Crowd cheers louder. NINO moves away from the window, ANGELO stays.*

Let's get away from this window before I start throwing furniture at them.

ANGELO

I wanna watch some more.

> *NINO walks up to ANGELO wraps his arms around him.*

NINO

(*seductively*) Come on …

ANGELO
What.

NINO
Come on … I wanna show you my own version of gay
pride.

> *NINO slaps ANGELO on the butt and walks towards the
> doorway that leads to their bedroom.*

ANGELO
Oooooh! We're finally admitting it?

> *NINO sensually takes off his shirt.*

NINO
Only in the bedroom.

> *NINO exits, ANGELO follows him. Then to the audience,
> smiling:*

ANGELO
Only in the bedroom.

> *Crowds cheer loudest. Crossfade to:*

Scene 3: Café

> *ANNA, Angelo's sister, sits at a table, smoking cigarettes
> and drinking espresso at break-neck speed. ANGELO
> arrives, they kiss, a peck on both cheeks. ANGELO sits.
> ANNA extends her hand.*

ANNA
Did you get me the Valium?

> *ANGELO hands her the Valium.*

ANGELO
Here … what's the big crisis?

ANNA pops a pill.

ANNA

    Our parents. They were having an argument about who
    died the more violent death: Aunt Yolanda or Uncle
    Domenic ... I'm telling you Angelo, ever since *papa*
    retired, all they do is scream at each other! I can't take
    it anymore!

    ANNA pops another pill.

ANGELO

    And that's why you're moving out.

ANNA

    Yeah—No, that didn't work out.

ANGELO

    But you rented an apartment.

ANNA

    There was no light in that place. All the windows faced
    an alley. And the neighbors were *so* noisy.

ANGELO

    How could you tell the neighbors were noisy?

ANNA

    Just by looking at them.

ANGELO

    Just by looking at them?

ANNA

    (*shouting*) I can tell if someone's noisy just by looking
    at them in the face! Okay?

ANGELO

    (*shouting*) Okay! (*beat*) Shhh!

ANNA

    Shh! How's Nino?

ANGELO
  He's fine.

ANNA
  You're so lucky to have a lover. What I wouldn't give to
  have some man drool all over me.

ANGELO
  You can have a man drool all over you if you wanted.

ANNA
  Nah, I only meet losers.

ANGELO
  You're never together long enough to know whether
  they're losers or not.

ANNA
  You can tell after the first time you sleep with someone
  if they're a loser or not. Besides, I don't want a steady
  relationship.

ANGELO
  But you just said that ...

ANNA
  (*upset, quickly*) I know what I just said Angelo I don't
  need you to tell me what I just said. I said it so I know
  what I said! Okay!?!

ANGELO
  Open your mouth.

    ANNA opens her mouth. ANGELO pops a Valium in.

ANNA
  Grazie!

ANGELO
  Prego. Man, you really are screwed up.

ANNA
Tell me something I don't know. And by the way, so are
you.

ANGELO
I am not.

ANNA
Oh no? ... how's your "roommate" Nino?

ANGELO
That's not being screwed up. That's just being in the
closet.

ANNA
And being in the closet is screwed up. Studies prove it.

Bulls-eye. ANGELO pops a Valium. Beat.

ANGELO
Anna.

ANNA
What?

ANGELO
How do you think our parents would react if I were to
tell them.

ANNA
Tell them what?

ANGELO
You know that I'm ... a ...

ANNA
A FAG? What are you retarded? No way are you gonna
tell them!

ANGELO
But you just said that being in the closet is ...

ANNA

Screwed-up … it is, but I live with our parents. *I'm* the one who's gonna have to deal with their melodramatics 24/7. Besides, *mamma* still hasn't recovered from poor Aunt Yolanda's death.

ANGELO

She died thirty years ago!

ANNA

(*made her point*) Yeah!

ANGELO

So what do you think? This is gonna kill them?

ANNA

Yes, this is gonna kill them.

Beat. ANNA *smiling an evil smile:*

Tell 'em!

Crossfade to:

Scene 4: Maria and Gino's House

ANGELO has just told his parents. GINO and MARIA pace frantically from the dining room to the living room.

MARIA

I want you to go see a doctor, *immediatamente.*

GINO

I survived the war for this?

MARIA

I want you to move out of downtown.

GINO

The years I sacrificed to buy this house in St. Leonard, and now, no one wants to live here!

MARIA

I want you to go to confession.

GINO

Abbi fortuna e dormi! Good luck, sleep tight. How come I never had any good luck?

MARIA

You had plenty of luck, you just never took advantage of it.

GINO

Don't you start with me Maria!

MARIA

My son just told me he's an *omosessuale*, I gotta start with somebody, Gino!

ANGELO

Ma, you're being ridiculous.

GINO

Don't you call your mother ridiculous!

MARIA

(*to GINO*) You had to wait for your son to tell us he was a *finocchio* to start defending me?

ANGELO

(*exasperated*) Everything will be okay.

MARIA

From this day on, nothing will be okay.

GINO

(*to ANGELO*) Go to your room!

ANGELO
You turned my room into a den.

MARIA
Didn't I tell you to leave that room alone?

GINO
You have never supported me!

MARIA
I have never supported *YOU*?

GINO
When I wanted him to join the hockey team, what did you say?

MARIA
He don't like sports.

GINO
That would have made him normal!

MARIA
Why I had to live to hear this, I don't know.

GINO
Look at what you're doing to your *mamma*!

MARIA
Gino, I can't feel my arm.

GINO
Don't die on me, Maria!

MARIA
I think my time has come.

GINO
(*to ANGELO*) You killed your own *mamma*!

ANGELO
She's not dying!

MARIA

(*shouting*) I don't need *you* to tell *me* if I'm dying!

GINO

I think it's best for you to leave this house, and go back to the village.

ANGELO

I don't live in the village!

MARIA

What village?

GINO

The *omosessuale* village.

MARIA

(*baffled*) There's an *omosessuale* village?

GINO

On St. Catherine Street, between Beaudry and Papineau.

MARIA

Hey! How come you know so much about this village?

GINO

I know a lot more than you think!

MARIA

Yeah. But an *omosessuale village*?

GINO

Are you saying I'm a *omosessuale*?

ANGELO

Oh God.

GINO

Because if that's what you're saying, Maria, I don't wanna hear it!

MARIA

Well, he's gotta get it from somebody!

GINO

Basta! I'm leaving … Angelo, I'll be sleeping on your couch.

ANGELO

You will?

MARIA

No. You have a bad back. Nino will sleep on the couch.

ANGELO

(*to his father*) You can stay in the guest room, if you want.

MARIA & GINO

What guest room?

ANGELO

Nino and I sleep in the same bed.

> *A beat. MARIA and GINO are awestruck.*

MARIA

I had to live this long to hear this?

GINO

Hockey! Hockey! The answer was hockey!

MARIA

Don't you put all the blame on me!

GINO

And don't you put it on me!

GINO & MARIA

(*looking up*) Dio Mio! Perché noi?

> *GINO and MARIA freeze.*

ANGELO

(*to the audience*) I knew they suspected.

> *Crossfade to:*

Scene 5: Angelo and Nino's Apartment

Wash comes up as ANGELO enters. NINO is sitting on the couch, livid. ANGELO puts his arms around NINO. NINO pulls away.

NINO
Don't you touch me!

ANGELO
What?

NINO
Why did you have to go and tell them.

ANGELO
I don't know. I was with my sister, and she was so screwed up and she said that I was too, and I thought, Jesus, I am, and we were doing Valium and next thing I know …

NINO
(*shouting, serious*) I can't believe you did this without talking to me first.

ANGELO
Coming out is a good thing. Studies prove it.

NINO
We always agreed that no one was to know about this relationship except you and me!

ANGELO
I know. What can I tell you? I did it. And now it's done.

NINO
Who else are you gonna tell?

ANGELO
No one.

NINO

These things spread.

ANGELO

It's not gonna spread. You think my parents want people to know that their son is a fag?

NINO

(*worried*) Did your mother say she was gonna tell my mother?

ANGELO

Your mother! That's why you find the closet so warm and comfy.

NINO

Never mind! Did she?

ANGELO

No and she's not gonna. Look … my parents took it relatively well.

NINO

Yeah right.

ANGELO

Just don't eat anything my mother offers you when we go over.

NINO

They threatened to kill me?

ANGELO

No, but they *are* Italian.

NINO

Stop shitting on Italians.

ANGELO

I don't shit on Italians.

NINO

You're the classic self-hating Italian.

ANGELO

I am not!

NINO

Please, the way you portray Italians in your plays ... it's disgraceful.

ANGELO

The truth hurts.

NINO

Italians have greatly contributed to civilization. We have given the world Michaelangelo, Fellini, the pizza—

ANGELO

—Mussolini, the Mafia, garlic breath.

> *NINO, worried ,not really listening to the conversation interrupts ANGELO with:*

NINO

My mother is gonna find out now, and—

ANGELO

—Nino, you're over thirty, you're an accountant; don't you think it's time you cut the pasta strings?

NINO

Another jab at Italians. One more and I'm outta here.

ANGELO

But of course you don't wanna disappoint *mammina*! No, no, except for the fact that you're queer, you did everything to please her: You went to university. Became a nice little accountant ...

NINO

I'm not gonna count that as a jab.

ANGELO
The only thing missing is for you to marry some big-haired, small-minded Mary Minghia, move into the apartment directly above your mommy's and have a bunch of kids that your *mammina* can babysit, while you and your lovely Italian bimbo wife are out greatly contributing to western civilization!

At a loss for words NINO storms out.

Wait a minute … Nino. Nino?

Door slams.

ANGELO
Shit!

Wash crossfades to:

Scene 6: Crescent Street Bar

Note: Crescent is an ultra-straight bawdy downtown Montreal street where many Americans and Italians hang out.

NINO is sitting at a table on a stool. PINA, late-twenties, very attractive, big hair, walks in, sipping a drink. Loud "Bar" music plays. PINA looks at NINO. He ignores her. She is about to leave when she hones in on him and says:

PINA
Excuse me, aren't you Joe Pietracoupa?

NINO
No.

PINA

Sorry. (*about to leave, then*) Didn't you go to Pius Ten
High School?

NINO

I did go to Pius, yes.

> *PINA immediately goes and sit on the stool next to NINO.*

PINA

That's where I know you from. Weren't you
homecoming king?

NINO

(*a bit embarrassed*) I was, yes.

PINA

Wait! Don't tell me … Dino!

NINO

Nino.

PINA

Mastronomo.

NINO

Paventi.

PINA

I'm so stupid, of course. Nino Paventi! You were
homecoming king with my best friend Franca Della
Rovere!

NINO

Franca! It's been years! How is Franca?

PINA

Married … two kids …

> *PINA starts to cry.*

NINO

(*uncomfortable*) What's wrong?

PINA

I should be married too by now!

NINO

Broken engagement?

PINA

I never even came close to being engaged, me.

NINO

(*uncomfortable*) I didn't get your name.

PINA

(*wiping tears*) Pina ... Pina Lunetti.

NINO

Nice to meet you, Pina.

PINA

That's what they all say. Nice to meet you Pina! Then
do I ever hear from them again? No!

Pina's cell-phone rings. She reaches for it, still sniffling.

Aw shit! (*answers phone, assertive*) Lunetti! ... Whaddya
mean Moretti didn't show up? ... Listen, the contract
says today and I want them today so if Moretti isn't
there with his fuckin' doors, it's his ass in a sling, along
with yours! *Capito*?!? Good!

PINA closes the cell phone and puts it back in her purse.

NINO

(*impressed*) Wow!

PINA

Oh. Impossible to get good people to work for you
nowadays!

NINO

What do you do?

PINA
I run my father's construction company.

NINO
Wait a minute ... Lunetti, that's where I recognize the
name from ... you're Lunetti—?

PINA & NINO
Constructions!

PINA nods.

NINO
(*impressed*) You built most of the houses in my old
neighborhood.

PINA
R.D.P.? That's us.

NINO
I'm impressed.

PINA
Don't be ... Me I been around it all my life. After my
father had his heart attack, I took over.

NINO
You run this company all by yourself?

PINA
Yeah—my good-for-nothing brother used to run it with
me. But he liked to work from the Casino, so me I gave
him the boot! You're not married?

NINO
Uh ... No.

PINA
(*gets up*) But you have a girlfriend.

NINO
Me? No, no.

33

Pina's interest is piqued.

PINA

How come? All the girls at school we always said that you'd be the first to get married 'cause you're such a hunk!

NINO

(*uncomfortable*) Thanks.

PINA goes back to her seat.

PINA

What do you do?

NINO

I'm an accountant.

PINA

Gimme your card. We can always use good accountants.

NINO

I don't have my card with me.

PINA

(*handing him her card*) You should always carry your business card with you. Everyone is a potential client you know.

NINO

I kind of left home in a rush.

PINA

Argument with your mom?

NINO

Actually, I live on my own.

PINA

Why? Are your parents dead?

NINO

Only my father.

PINA

Who takes care of your mother?

NINO

She does.

PINA

Oh. (*changing subjects*) Do you have a car?

NINO

Sure.

PINA

Maybe we could take a ride ... to your apartment.

NINO

To my apartment?

PINA

We could talk some more.

NINO

Listen Pina, I have a houseguest so ...

PINA

Then we can talk in the car ... Me I'm used to it.

NINO

I'm gonna have to pass.

PINA

You don't need to draw me a picture ... You think I'm ugly. What else is new?

NINO

No, I'm just late for something.

PINA

Sure. Listen, if you want, gimme a call. Number's on the card.

> *Cell-phone rings again.*

Managgia! (*answers*) Lunetti! … Moretti you idiot, where the hell are you? You said the doors were gonna be delivered today and I want them today!

> *As PINA talks on the phone, NINO gets up. She waves "good-bye." NINO looks at her go: what a woman! He exits and as lights fade:*

Ma che cazzo fai? You think I'm an idiot or what? *Cornuto, disgraziato, figlio di putana!* Awww FUCK YOU MORETTI! Shit!

> *Crossfade to:*

Scene 7: Gino and Maria's House

GINO
> (*by the entrance*) Lina, *avanti, avanti.*

> *LINA PAVENTI, Nino's mother, early to late sixties, enters. LINA also speaks with an Italian accent.*

LINA
> (*arms extended for a hug*) Gino, you big fat *stronzo*, how are you, ah?

> *They hug and kiss hello.*

GINO
> *Si tira avanti.* We must go on.

LINA
> No matter what, or we croak! Where's that *stonata* wife of yours?

GINO
> She's in the kitchen, where all women should be.

LINA

Gino, you slimy bastard, if I weren't such a *signora* I'd kick your balls right back to Naples!

LINA and GINO laugh. MARIA enters.

Maria! Maria! *Faccia brutta, come stai?*

MARIA and LINA kiss hello.

MARIA

Bene, bene. (*to GINO*) Did you offer her something to drink yet?

GINO

No.

MARIA

What are you waiting for?

GINO

(*to LINA*) What can I offer you?

LINA

My husband's been dead eighteen years. What I need most you can't offer, 'cause you're married.

GINO

We can always make arrangements. Mari, what do you say? Lemme help out an old friend.

MARIA

(*to LINA*) You're better off with your memories.

(*shouting, to GINO*) Didn't I tell you to go get Lina a drink?!

GINO

(*to LINA*) What can I get you?

LINA
Nothing fancy. A little scotch and soda on the rocks.
Forget the rocks, go easy on the soda, and have a ball
with the scotch.

GINO
(*to MARIA*) And for you, *amore?*

MARIA
A glass of water.

GINO
I'll be right back.

> *GINO exits. Beat. MARIA and LINA sit in the living
> room. They smile at each other, uncomfortably. MARIA to
> break the silence:*

MARIA
Terrible weather, ah?

LINA
Fa schifo.

> *MARIA smiles, what's taking her husband so long?*

LINA
So, tell me Maria. What's wrong? What's this urgent
matter you had to discuss with me today?

MARIA
Your son.

LINA
(*in a panic*) NINO!?! Give it to me straight Maria, what
happened to my son?

MARIA
Nothing!

> *LINA is relieved. GINO enters, tray of drinks in hand.*

GINO

The bar is open!

Each take a drink. They toast:

EVERYBODY

Cin cin, alla salute!

They all take a sip.

LINA

Okay. Now suppose you tell me what the hell this is all about.

MARIA

(*to GINO*) You tell her.

GINO

Why me?

MARIA

You got more diplomacy.

GINO

You always say I was raised like a pig.

MARIA

Please don't aggravate me right now.

GINO

I'M aggravating *YOU?*

MARIA

(*shouting*) Yes! You're aggravating me!

LINA

Kids, kids come on. Whatever it is, I'm sure we can work it out.

GINO

Lina with all due respect, this is between me and my wife.

MARIA

What are you talking about? This involves her son.

LINA

What about my son?

GINO

Your son—is a—miserable son-of-a- bitch! No offence.

LINA

Hey hey! ... where do you come off calling my son a son-of-a-bitch, you cootie-filled bastard!

GINO

You don't know what your son did!

MARIA

Don't blame her son ... Who's to say it's not our son?

GINO

I'm to say it's not our son!

LINA

What about my son!?! Can someone please tell me?!!

MARIA

I'm sorry to have to break it to you this way.

GINO

Your son's a homo.

> Beat. MARIA gives her husband a "you stupid idiot"
> look. LINA is dumbfounded.

LINA

My son's a what?

GINO

And he turned our Angelo into one too.

LINA

Are you saying my son Nino has been banging your son Angelo?

GINO

No. (*beat*) It's the other way around.

MARIA

What does it matter?

LINA

(*insulted*) Excuse me sir, but if anyone is not being banged here, it's my Nino.

GINO

What makes you say Nino is doing the banging?

LINA

'Cause Nino's a banger!

GINO

And Angelo isn't?

LINA

No!

GINO

I'm gonna have to ask you to leave!

LINA

Lina Paventi does not get asked to leave. Lina Paventi leaves, you sick pervert.

MARIA

We haven't discussed anything of importance here!

LINA

What's to discuss? You get me over here to tell me that your son has been banging my son. That's a sick lie, so, *finita la discussione!* Thank you very much for the *dollar-store scotch,* and *arrivederci!*

ANNA *walks in.*

ANNA

(*pleasant*) *Buon giorno Signora Paventi, come va?*

LINA

Va fa 'nculo!

LINA storms out.

ANNA

Oh-kay!

ANNA is about to leave when:

MARIA

Wait a minute Anna, we have something very
important to tell you.

They lead her to the couch. ANNA is panicked.

GINO

You better sit down.

ANNA

What is it *mamma?*

MARIA

(*solemn*) Your brother.

ANNA

(*panicked*) Angelo! What happened to Angelo?

GINO

(*more solemn*) He's a *omosessuale.*

A beat. Then ANNA relieved:

ANNA

Oh phew! I know.

MARIA

(*surprised*) You know?

GINO

How long have you known?

MARIA

Why didn't you tell us?

42

GINO

What else are you keeping from us?

MARIA

(*pulling on Anna's hair*) Didn't I teach you not to lie?

ANNA

I didn't lie, you never asked!

MARIA

Why would Angelo tell her and not us!

ANNA

Will you two calm down! (*compassionate, smiling*) Yes,
Angelo is gay. All you have to do is accept it, and give
him all your love.

    GINO and MARIA are aghast.

GINO

Go to your room!

    ANNA laughs.

ANNA

I'm way too old to be sent to my room!

MARIA

(*shouting*) Your father told you to go to your room!
Subito!

    A beat.

ANNA

(*shouting*) Okay!

    ANNA exits. Crossfade to:

Scene 8: Angelo and Nino's Apartment

ANGELO is working on his laptop. Looks at his watch. He continues working. NINO enters.

ANGELO
Where you been?

NINO
Out.

ANGELO
Out where?

NINO
What's it to you?

ANGELO
What's it to me? You're my boyfriend.

NINO
Oh yeah right and we tell each other everything. I forgot.

ANGELO
Okay. I know where this is leading and, you're gonna be really happy with what I did.

NINO
Another surprise. Just what I needed.

ANGELO
No this is good because you see, I called Anna, and I told her to tell my parents not to tell your mother.

NINO
That's it?

ANGELO
Well yeah. Isn't that great news? Your mother's never gonna know!

NINO is not impressed.

NINO

I'll be in my room, and don't come around.

NINO exits.

ANGELO

Aw come on, Nino, not your room. Nino! *Nino!* Shit!

ANGELO grabs his jacket and exits the apartment. The phone rings.

NINO

(*off-stage*) You gonna get that?

NINO enters the room, phone continues to ring.

Angelo? Angelo?

The answering machine picks up:

ANSWERING MACHINE

(*ANGELO's voice*) We can't come to the phone right now

(*NINO's voice*) But if you leave your name and number after the beep

(*ANGELO's voice*) We'll call you back.

(*ANGELO and NINO's voice*) Ciaaaoooo!

NINO

(*mimicking*) Ciaaaaaaoooo!!

Machine beeps. It's ANNA.

ANNA

(*voiceover*) Nino, it's Anna, my mom told your mom. Head for the hills! *Ciao.*

NINO

Fuck!

> *He grabs a jacket, heads for the door, and comes face to face with LINA.*

LINA

Going somewhere?

NINO

Mamma! How'd you get in here? The door's locked, the alarm's on …

LINA

(*matter-of-factly*) I'm Sicilian.

> *LINA raises her arms. NINO drops his jacket to protect his face with his hands. LINA hugs her son.*

NINO

(*uncomfortable*) So, did you talk to …

LINA

(*letting go of her son*) *Si, Si.*

NINO

So then you know about …

LINA

I know, I know, I know everything.

NINO

And you're not …

LINA

Sicuro che no, you're my son, I love you. I forgive everything. (*a beat*) Now come on, pack your bags and let's get the hell outta here! *Andiamo!*

NINO

What?

LINA

I forgive everything. You'll go to confession, and the big Man upstairs will forgive too. Now where's your luggage, I'll help you pack.

NINO

Ma, what are you doing?

LINA

We're going home.

NINO

I am home.

LINA

Oh no. This is not your home. Now come on; I made a big batch of cannelloni, and your Uncle Guido brought us a gallon of his *vino* to wash it down with.

NINO

Cannelloni and wine? That's supposed to make me leave …

LINA

(*upset*) I'm doing the best I can! I'm welcoming you back with open arms. What more do you want?

NINO

Listen ma, I'm sorry you had to learn this the way you did, I should have told you …

LINA

There's nothing to tell, this was a—phase.

NINO

Ma …

LINA

(*firm and loud*) *Antonino*! If you don't follow me outta here right now, you are no longer my son!

> Beat.

NINO
You don't mean that.

LINA
No. I don't. You're the only kid I got ... look at you, the spitting image of your father.

(*melodramatic*) Thank God death spared him all of this ... Come on, let's go home Nino.

NINO
I am home.

LINA
(*upset*) Are you telling me that you are choosing to stay here rather than come back with your mother who sacrificed her life to raise you?

NINO
I'm not choosing anyone over anyone else.

LINA
Zito! If you don't want me to smack you in the face, don't say another word.

NINO
But—

LINA
(*upset*) Not another Goddamn word! I'm gonna go now. You want some cannelloni, you come with me! You want some ... disgusting, mortal sin activity ... you stay here!

Just then, ANGELO enters. He freezes when he sees LINA.

LINA
Well, if it isn't "the wife."

ANGELO and NINO do not know how to react.

ANGELO
(*meekly*) How are you *Signora Paventi*?

48

LINA

(*smiling*) How sweet. How am I? Eh. How am I?

> *LINA walks towards ANGELO. ANGELO steps back. LINA gently grabs Angelo's face.*

Look at this beautiful face! Ah Nino? Nice, eh! Now think of his big fat father. That's the face you're gonna end up with!

> *LINA storms out. ANGELO and NINO stare at each other. Crossfade to:*

Scene 9: Gino and Maria's House

Special on ANNA who is sipping a glass of wine.

ANNA

(*to the audience*) Mmmmm! My father's home-made wine. The best ... They always wanted what was best for us, my mother and father. The best clothes, the best schools, the best food ... My mother's cooking ... now that was true art. A dash of this a pinch of that, and— Mmmmm ecstasy! I can still smell the tomato sauce simmering on Sunday mornings. We'd get up just in time to make the ten o'clock mass, after which the whole neighborhood gathered to discuss what kind of pasta they'd be eating for lunch ... But I knew that my mom's was the best. And you should see the feasts this woman put together for family gatherings! Antipasto, pasta, meat course, vegetables from our garden, dessert ... enough to feed all my perpetually starved cousins and aunts and uncles, and their cousins and aunts and uncles who'd come to these rambunctious gatherings. (*smiles*) You can't begin to imagine the chaos that reigned at these parties. The screaming, the shouting, the laughing. Everybody speaking at the same time and no one listening to each other. And my Aunt Yolanda blasting her music, trying to teach everyone how to do the mambo. But no one was ever game … What chaos! What beautiful, serene chaos. (*beat*) It's funny you know, as much as I blame these people for all my neuroses, I can't think of a time when I was happier than at those Sunday dinners … (*beat*) I think the problem with us Italians is that once we enter the outside world, the chaos we encounter is not laced with any serenity: when someone shouts at you, they're *really* shouting at you! And the food out here, well, it's just something that's eaten on the run to sustain your energy. There's no (*searching for the right word*) … art involved. (*beat*) What I wouldn't give to hear my mother screaming …

MARIA

(*from offstage*) Anna! Supper!

ANNA

(*smiles*) It's as if she were here.

MARIA

(*offstage, shouting*) It's getting cold!

ANNA

(*drops her smile, to audience*) Oh, I forgot, she really is here. Excuse me.

MARIA

(*offstage shouting*) Anna!

ANNA

(*shouting*) Okay! Okay! I'm not deaf!

> *Crossfade to general wash. MARIA and GINO are sitting at the dining room table, eating. ANNA joins them.*

MARIA
> You're too busy to help me set the table, but you're not
> too busy to have a glass of wine before dinner.

GINO
> If she wants to have a glass of wine before dinner let
> her have a glass of wine before dinner.

MARIA
> (*to GINO*) Just like your side of the family, always with a
> drink in her hand.

ANNA
> This is my first drink of the day!

MARIA
> (*to ANNA*) Your Uncle Domenic died because of his
> heavy drinking, you know.

GINO
> My brother Domenic died of lung cancer. (*to ANNA*)
> It's your Aunt Yolanda who drowned in a tub of   .

MARIA
> (*shouting*) My sister never touched a drink in her life!

GINO
> (*shouting*) Oh yeah?

MARIA
> (*shouting*) Yeah!

> *Beat.*

ANNA
> (*to MARIA*) Is this "Buitoni" pasta?

MARIA
> Yes, isn't it delicious?

GINO
> It's the best!

MARIA pours more wine in Anna's glass. GINO serves MARIA more pasta. Slow fade to black as the three eat their meal. Crossfade to:

Scene 10: Angelo and Nino's Apartment

Wash comes up. Romantic music plays. NINO sits on the couch watching television. ANGELO enters. He approaches NINO, stands behind him. ANGELO puts his arms around NINO. NINO shakes his head "no." ANGELO moves away. Beat. ANGELO tries again. NINO moves away. Beat. ANGELO tries again. NINO sighs. ANGELO massages Nino's arms. NINO closes his eyes. Opens them. Stares into Angelo's eyes. A sullen, lonely stare. He then rubs his head against Angelo's arms. ANGELO kisses NINO. NINO grabs ANGELO by the back of the head. They kiss on the lips. ANGELO pulls Nino's shirt off. They continue kissing. NINO pulls ANGELO down on the couch. The kissing becomes more passionate. NINO pulls Angelo's shirt off. A heavy make-out session ensues. Hands, tongues, lips, probe each other's bodies. Sometimes softly, sometimes violently. Like two lovers who haven't seen each other in a long while. Like two lovers who are reconciling after a fight. Light slowly fades to blackout, as the two are about to make love.

Scene 11: Gino and Maria's House

General wash comes up. GINO sits on the sofa, clutching his chest. He is suffering from severe heartburn. MARIA enters, mug in hand. She hands it to GINO.

MARIA

Here. Drink your *cammomila*, it will make you feel better.

GINO

Nothing will make me feel better. No more Buitoni pasta for me!

MARIA

No more Buitoni pasta, no more oregano, no more garlic ... you better start fixing your own meals, 'cause I dunno what to give you no more!

GINO

It's never been this bad before. What do you think this is, Mari?

MARIA

What it's always been: nerves! Just like the doctor said. There's nothing wrong with your stomach.

GINO

It feels like someone lit a match and shoved it in here. I don't know how much more of this I can take.

MARIA

Calma! You just need to keep calm.

GINO

(*shouting*) How can I keep calm? My whole life has been one big disappointment after another.

MARIA

That's all you know how to do: feel sorry about the way your life turned out. You think I'm having such a great time here?

GINO

Didn't I make you happy, Mari?

MARIA

Si you made me happy! Now stop being stupid and drink your *cammomila*!

Beat.

GINO

Maria, there's something I gotta tell you.

MARIA

(*worried*) What Gi? What is it.

GINO

When I was working at the shop there were a couple of guys we thought were, you know (*does the limp wrist thing*) … and we always made fun of them. This thing with Angelo, you think this is payback?

MARIA

All these crazy ideas you got in your head! That's why your stomach's sick! (*a beat*) We should call Angelo.

GINO

We should!

Beat.

Mari, do we still love him?

MARIA

What kind of a question is that? Of course we still love him! He's still our beautiful Angelo!

GINO

But if we still love him, and if he's still our beautiful
Angelo, how come we find it so hard to pick up the
phone?

MARIA

I dunno.

GINO

But ...

MARIA

(*defensive*) I dunno, Gi, I just don't know. I'm going to
bed, call me if you need anything. Okay? *Buona Notte*!

> *GINO nods "yes." MARIA exits. Crossfade to:*

Scene 12: Cemetery

> *LINA kneels in front of her husband's tombstone. She
> cleans the tombstone, kisses it, sits down and to the
> tombstone:*

LINA

How you doing, Frankie ... Me? Can't complain. A
little arthritis creeping up these old legs but besides
you not being with me anymore, I'm okay ... You been
good Frankie? I have. Haven't touched no one since
you left. Not that I haven't gotten any offers. I'm still a
woman Frankie ... A woman ... Hey! You better be
staying away from that *putana* Teresa Iasenza! What am
I thinking? Of course you're staying away. You're in
heaven, and Teresa's in hell. (*beat*) I miss you
something awful Frankie. I try to keep up the sense of
humour that used to make you laugh so much, but I'm
not as funny anymore. And this is why. Seeing you six
feet under, that's the reason why. (*notices something*)

What the hell is that lying in your flowers?
(*gets up, shocked*) What the ... *Madonna Mia*! Frankie!
(*she takes a Kleenex, picks up "the thing lying in his flowers":
a used condom*)

They desecrated your grave! (*shouting, running around
waving the condom*) What happened to respect for the
dead, ah?

> *LINA doesn't know what to do with the condom. She
> decides to shove it in her bag.*

The things that go on in the world today, Frankie.
Everything's outta control! ... Nino? Nino's fine. He's
going through this ... phase. But don't worry about it.
It's not his fault! He'll come back to me ... Yeah, he
left home about a year ago. I didn't tell you 'cause I
didn't wanna upset you, but they say the dead see
everything ... *Dio Mio*! I hope you weren't watching
when he and his friend were ... This would've never
happened if you were still around, you bastard!—I miss
you Frankie. Did I say that already? Well I'm gonna say
it again and again. Because the more time passes,
Frankie, the more I miss you.

> *LINA takes out a Kleenex and wipes a tear. MARIA
> enters. She notices LINA. She is disconcerted. She tries to
> walk by her without being noticed, but Lina's crying
> makes it impossible for MARIA to just walk by.*

MARIA
   Lina.

LINA
   (*wipes her tears*) What the hell are you doing here?

MARIA
   I came to see my sister. Four graves down.

LINA

Your sister's dead?

MARIA

You even came to the funeral.

LINA

Oh yeah. Yolanda. The one who "accidentally" fell off a bridge.

MARIA

(*upset*) What was that?

LINA

What was what?

MARIA

(*imitates LINA*) "Accidentally," like the accident wasn't really an accident.

LINA

Who says it wasn't?

MARIA

Plenty of people.

LINA

And I'm not one of them.

Beat. MARIA goes and stands next to LINA.

MARIA

Frankie's looking good.

LINA

Thank you. See the statue? Imported from Italy. A little surprise for his birthday.

MARIA

Who's that?

LINA

Sant' Arturo!

MARIA
>I never heard of him.

LINA
>Just 'cause you never heard of him, doesn't mean he don't exist.

MARIA
>What's he the patron saint of?

LINA
>How the hell am I supposed to know? I thought he'd look good on the tombstone.

MARIA
>He does; he matches with the grey. Isn't it disgusting the way they keep this place?

LINA
>Look at what I found on my Frankie!

>*LINA takes out the used condom.*

MARIA
>(*gasps*) *Madonna mia! Ack!*

>(*puzzled*) And why you keep it?

LINA
>(*shouting, looking around*) I'm gonna put the evil eye on this bastard's sperm! Make this *cornuto* wish he were impotent!

>*LINA puts the condom back in the bag.*

MARIA
>I don't know what this world is coming to!

LINA
>That's what I was telling my Frankie. Everything's outta control.

MARIA
Outta control! Si. Si. Si.

A beat.

LINA
Have you spoken to …

MARIA
No. You?

LINA
My door is always open. But he chooses not to come in!

MARIA
Mine too.

LINA
I miss my Nino so much.

MARIA
I miss my Angelo too.

LINA
You think we should make the first move?

MARIA
Certo. But how do we move?

LINA
Very carefully. We can start with a little get together.

MARIA
Yes! Supper at my place!

LINA
Or at my place.

MARIA
But my place is bigger.

LINA
Yes, but my place is nicer.

MARIA takes off. LINA stops her.

LINA

Maria! Maria! Please. Sit down. I'm sorry ... this whole thing with Nino has got me all nervous.

MARIA

(*sits down*) I don't sleep anymore. Can you sleep?

LINA

I sleep. It's the nervous diarrhea that's killing me.

MARIA

That's awful.

LINA

It's not very pretty, but what can you do? ... Listen Mari, the kids ... this is a phase they're going through, right?

MARIA

I don't know.

LINA

I hear that a lot of guys go through this when they're teenagers.

MARIA

They're grown men.

LINA

They're late that's all. So I'm thinking, we have a little dinner party at your place. You provide the food, and I bring along this nice Italian girl I know.

MARIA

What for?

LINA

For Angelo. Is Anna seeing anybody?

MARIA
   No.

LINA
   Good. She'd be perfect for Nino. If he fell for the
   brother, he might fall for the sister.

MARIA
   Lina this sounds crazy, no offence.

LINA
   None taken. Is a week from Saturday good for you?

MARIA
   Yes ...

LINA
   Then a week from Saturday it is ... I'm so happy we're
   friends again!

   LINA hugs a skeptical MARIA. Crossfade to:

Scene 13: Crescent Street Bar

   *Same place as Pina and Nino's first meeting. "Bar"
   music plays. NINO is sitting at the bar looking around.
   PINA enters, sees NINO, goes up to him.*

PINA
   Me, I don't know if I should talk to you.

NINO
   (*happy to see her*) Pina hi! How are you ... sit!

PINA
   (*skeptical*) How come you never called me?

NINO
   I've been meaning to ...

PINA

You don't have to make excuses. You're not interested in me, that's all.

NINO

No ...

PINA

It's okay. Me, I'm used to it.

NINO

No, no— I do like you.

PINA

Ay! I don't need your pity.

NINO

This isn't pity. Come on sit. Sit Pina. Please.

PINA

(*yeah, right attitude*) You really like me?

NINO

Actually, I came here hoping that I might bump into you.

PINA

Even after the stupid way I acted last time ... bawling my eyes out like an idiot.

NINO

I don't think you acted stupid.

PINA

Yeah, well ...

Pina's cell-phone starts to ring.

Shit!

PINA decides to ignore it. It eventually stops ringing.

NINO

You're not gonna get that?

PINA

No ... let them figure out what to do. Let them see what it's like without the stupid bitch to bail them out ... That's what they call me behind my back ... stupid bitch. Cute, huh?

NINO

Why do you put up with it?

PINA

What am I gonna do? Fire them all? You gotta put up with the hand life deals you. Me I got dealt with the job from hell, so ...

NINO

(*puzzled*) The job from hell? But you're ...

PINA

Lunetti Constructions, I know, I know ...

NINO

You make it sound like this wasn't your first career choice.

PINA

First? Are you kidding me? It wasn't even my last. But who gets to do what they really want, ah?

NINO

What did you wanna do?

PINA

Forget about it, it's too stupid.

NINO

Tell me something ... why do you think everything you do is stupid.

PINA

Because it is! Okay?

NINO

Okay!
So you're not gonna tell me what your first career choice was?

PINA

No.

NINO

(*teasing nudging her*) Come on, come on—

PINA

Forget about it!

NINO

Please??? For me?

> *PINA cannot resist Nino's request.*

PINA

Fashion design, you happy?

NINO

What's so stupid about that?

PINA

I was pretty good at it too. Me, I'd spend hours in my room drawing outfits. One of my teachers in school told me I should go into it.

NINO

Why didn't you?

PINA

My father persuaded me to change my mind.

NINO

Your father?

PINA

I almost went to fashion school, but when my father
found out, he had a fit, he took all of my designs and
he dragged me down to the fireplace in our basement.
Then he lit a fire and he made me throw all my
drawings, one by one, into the fire ... (*sullen, pensive*)
And then he forced me to watch them burn ... Then
he said if he ever caught me drawing again, he'd throw
me in the fire.

NINO

What a bastard!

PINA

Hey! Don't talk about my father like that, okay?

NINO

But ...

PINA

(*defensive*) Look ... In life you gotta go for what you
know for sure is gonna work out. Me I had this huge
construction company to play around with. What was I
gonna do? Abandon everything my father had worked
for, and follow some stupid dream? I don't think so.

NINO

You should be doing what you really want.

PINA

What I really want is to get married and have kids.
What am I supposed to do? Go up to a perfect stranger
and ask him to marry me?

NINO

Don't live your life waiting for some man to come
sweep you off your feet.

PINA

Why don't you just come out and say it: No one's ever gonna love me because I'm too ugly!

NINO

No, you're not getting it.

PINA

I told you I was stupid.

NINO

(*exasperated, almost angry*) Will you stop saying that! Jesus! You're a beautiful, intelligent woman, who doesn't need some man to make her happy and—

> *Before NINO can finish his sentence, PINA grabs Nino's face and plants a big wet kiss on his lips.*

PINA

You could make me happy.

NINO

Wha …

PINA

You see? Stupid, stupid, stupid!

> *PINA starts to cry.*

NINO

I'm sorry, I'm … You took me by surprise … I …

> *NINO puts his arms around her.*

PINA

No … please.

NINO

What do you say we go for a ride in my car? Huh?

PINA

In your car, but—

NINO kisses PINA on the neck. Then the lips. The two kiss passionately. Crossfade to:

Scene 14: Gino and Maria's House

It is the night of the "get together." MARIA frantically sets the table.

MARIA
(*screaming*) Anna! Anna! Anna!

> *ANNA enters.*

ANNA
What *mamma?*

MARIA
They're gonna arrive any minute and this place is a mess. Can you give me a hand?

ANNA
Where's the mess?

MARIA
Everywhere! Where's your father?

ANNA
You sent him out to buy bread.

MARIA
What's taking him so long? ... Is that what you're wearing?

ANNA
Yes.

MARIA
Go change. And put on some make-up.

ANNA

What are you talking about? It's just Angelo and Nino coming over.

MARIA

(*shouting*) Will you stop making me nervous and do as I say!

ANNA

(*shouting back*) Okay!

ANNA is about to exit.

MARIA

(*softer tone*) Anna.

ANNA

Yes *mamma*?

MARIA

When you told your brother we wanted him over, was he excited?

ANNA

Sure.

MARIA

How is he? Is he eating right?

ANNA

He's fine, *mamma*, he's fine.

MARIA

How do I look? I want him to like how I look.

ANNA

Sei bellissima mamma!

MARIA smiles at her daughter then:

MARIA

And you, you look like shit, now go change.

ANNA

(*upset exiting*) *Non c'e la faccio piu! Non c'e la faccio proprio piu!*

> *ANNA exits, GINO enters, double plastic bag in hand, gives the bag to MARIA.*

GINO

Te ... il pane.

> *MARIA looks through the bag.*

MARIA

What is this? This is not what I asked you to get!

GINO

A dozen long paninis, a dozen round ones!

MARIA

I said two dozen long, and half a dozen round!

GINO

What's the difference? It's all made with the same dough!

MARIA

The dinner is ruined! I'm calling the whole thing off!

GINO

Good, because this was a lousy idea in the first place!

MARIA

Don't you wanna make peace with your son?

GINO

Yeah! But this whole scheme of yours and Lina's, it's crazy!

MARIA

You have a better idea?

GINO

Lemme get this straight: Angelo gets fixed up with some *putana* Lina brings over.

MARIA

(*defensive*) She is not a *putana*!

GINO

And Anna ends up with Nino?

MARIA

Shh! She doesn't know yet.

GINO

Mari, this is crazy!

> *Doorbell rings.*

MARIA

(*in a complete panic*) *Madonna mia*! They're here! Get the door! (*GINO exits to get the door.*) Anna! They're here! *Gesu mio aiuteci tu*! They're here! Anna!

> *ANNA enters, dressed to the nines. GINO enters followed by ANGELO and NINO. NINO is carrying a bottle of wine. MARIA runs to her son and hugging and kissing him:*

Figlio mio!

> *MARIA then goes to NINO, kisses him.*

Nino, *come stai?*

NINO

Bene signora Barbieri.

> *ANNA kisses her brother.*

ANNA

Hello.

ANNA kisses NINO. NINO gives the bottle of wine to GINO.

GINO

Grazie, grazie.

MARIA

Why did you bring wine? You know not to bring anything.

ANNA

Ma, it's common courtesy when you're invited to dinner to bring something.

MARIA

At a stranger's house maybe, but we're family.

ANGELO

Gimme the wine, pa. We'll take it home.

GINO

This is pretty good wine.

MARIA

Gino give him back his wine.

GINO

(*shouting*) If they wanna give us wine, let them give us wine!

MARIA

(*shouting*) Do you always have to yell at me?!

GINO

(*shouting*) I'M always yelling at YOU?

NINO

I'm sorry, the wine was my idea.

ANGELO

Don't apologize, this isn't about wine. Obviously this reconciliation is not working, so let's leave.

MARIA

No, please!

ANNA

(*to ANGELO*) Relax, they're doing their best.

ANGELO

That's what I'm afraid of …

ANNA

So. How about we all sit down. Ah?

MARIA

Si, Sit. That's a good idea. (*hitting GINO*) Why didn't you think of that?

> *Chaotic seating process ensues. They all sit. Short silence then everyone speaks these next five lines at the same time:*

MARIA

(*in unison*) Is it still raining?

GINO

(*in unison*) Lousy weather.

ANNA

(*in unison*) Nice jacket, Nino.

ANGELO

(*in unison*) No, it's stopped.

NINO

(*in unison*) Is that a new TV?

> *They all laugh. A beat. Then:*

GINO

So Nino, do you think the Canadiens have a chance this year?

> *MARIA thinks that is the dumbest question she ever heard.*

NINO

I have no idea.

MARIA

He's not interested in hockey.

NINO

I'm very interested.

GINO

Really?

ANGELO

Nino played hockey right through university. Always the star player.

MARIA, with a look of satisfaction, looks at her husband and says:

MARIA

So, I guess hockey isn't the answer, ah Gino?

GINO makes a face as if to say, shut up. A beat.

ANGELO

Okay, so are we gonna have the big discussion before or after supper?

NINO

My mother isn't even here yet.

MARIA

Discuss? What's to discuss?

NINO

Nothing!

GINO

We're gonna have a pleasant evening.

ANGELO

Pleasant evening, yes. If we don't talk about it, it doesn't exist, right?

NINO

Angelo.

ANGELO

Why are we pretending like this is just a normal
evening?

MARIA

Because your father and me we accept your, your—you
know what.

ANGELO

You accept my "you know what" so well that you can't
even bring yourself to call my "you know what" by its
proper name.

Doorbell rings.

MARIA & GINO

I'll get it!

MARIA and GINO exit.

ANNA

(*hitting ANGELO*) What's the matter with you?

NINO

This is a big step for them. Can't you find it in your
self-righteous heart to admit that?

ANNA

(*to ANGELO*) You want a Valium?

ANGELO

No ... Why are you all dressed up?

ANNA

Because ... I dunno.

MARIA and GINO followed by LINA enter.

LINA

> *Buona Sera,* everybody, *buona sera!*
> (*notices ANNA*) Oh! Anna! *Sempre cosi bella.* (*hugging ANNA*) Always so gorgeous look at you. (*turns ANNA toward NINO*) Look at her Nino. So young and beautiful. God I hate you for being so skinny! (*laughs*) Angelo! (*hugs ANGELO*) Angelo! What a handsome young man you turned out to be, who do you take after, ah? Both your mother and father look like Goddamn circus freaks!

> *LINA laughs. ANNA bellow laughs. GINO and MARIA smile. They are not amused.*

LINA

> Nino! (*grabs Nino's jaw, squeezes it hard*) Why haven't you called? Ah? Why don't you ever call your *povera* old *mamma?*

NINO

> 'Cause I'm scared?

> *LINA laughs, squeezes her son's jaw harder, then lets go.*

MARIA

> Where's your friend?

LINA

> Parking the car. You guys don't mind I brought her along? All alone on a Saturday night. Poor girl.

> *Doorbell rings.*

> That's her. Anna sweetheart, can you get that?

> *ANNA exits.*

> She's very shy. So I want you bastards to go easy on her.

> *ANNA enters followed by PINA. NINO is shocked.*

> Come in, *bella.*

PINA

Buona sera.

LINA

Everyone, this is …

PINA notices NINO. Her face lights up.

PINA

Nino!

NINO

(*trying to hide his terror*) Pina?

LINA

You two know each other?

PINA

Yes, Nino and me—

NINO

—went to the same high school.

ANGELO

Good ol' Pius Ten. Also known as Don Corleone Comprehensive High School.

NINO

Here we go again. That's not true.

ANGELO

Please. The few students who actually graduated went on to become drug dealers or hookers.

NINO

Of course *you* would hate it. Most of the students and the teachers were Italian, and we know how much you love Italians.

ANGELO

I'm sorry, I forgot the "don't-attack-Pius-Ten" rule. The best years of Nino's life.

PINA

Mine too. (*to ANGELO*) You went to Pius same time as us?

ANGELO

Unfortunately.

PINA

Then I should know you ... Wait don't tell me.

ANGELO

(*not wanting to play her game*) Angelo. Angelo Barbieri.

A beat then:

PINA

The fag?

All are shocked.

ANGELO

My past has come back to haunt me. Who knew it had such big hair?

PINA

(*to LINA*) This is the nice young man you wanted me to meet ... the fag?

ANGELO

(*puzzled*) Meet?

LINA

Pina honey ... I didn't know.

PINA

All of Pius knew!

ANGELO

Ma, what's going on here?

ANNA

Yeah, what is going on?

PINA

I'm going home.

LINA

You stay here.

MARIA

The roast is almost ready.

PINA

Come on Nino, let's go.

ANGELO

Hold on a second here. Go where?

PINA

None of your business.

ANGELO

(*to PINA*) Nino is my business.

PINA

Nino, what does he mean by that?

MARIA

(*to relieve tension*) The roast is ready. *Mangiamo*!

ANGELO

Nino, tell her what I mean by that.

NINO

We'll discuss this some other time.

PINA

Why some other time? What happened in the car, that was all pretend?

NINO

Pina …

LINA

What happened in the car?

NINO

    Angelo …

ANGELO

    What car?

PINA

    His car.

ANGELO

    (*to NINO*) Our car?

PINA

    (*to ANGELO*) Your car?

LINA

    His car, our car, anybody's car. What d'you do in the
    Goddamn car!

ANGELO

    (*to NINO*) Tell me what you did in our car.

PINA

    (*to NINO*) Why d'you need to tell *him* what we did in
    your car?

ANGELO

    (*to NINO*) Tell her why you need to tell me!

LINA

    Is somebody gonna tell us something, please!?!

NINO

    Everyone, just stay calm.

PINA

    (*to NINO*) Are you ashamed of what we did?

NINO

    Pina, this isn't a good time to discuss what we did.

LINA

    What? What? What did you did?

NINO
Mamma—

PINA
We made love!

> *Collective gasp except for LINA. A beat. LINA raises her fists in the air; victory! She screams:*

LINA
Yeeeeeeees!

> *Beat.*

ANGELO
(*to PINA*) You're a fucking liar!

PINA
Oh yeah? Tell him, Nino.

ANGELO
Nino?

> *Beat.*

(*shouting*) Nino?

NINO
(*to ANGELO, upset*) You brought this on yourself!

ANGELO
What!?!

NINO
You and your coming out!

PINA
Come out from where?

LINA
A phase.

ANGELO
Phase, again with this phase. Your son is gay!

PINA

No!

NINO

(*ready to pounce*) You fucking watch your mouth in front of my mother!

LINA

Yeah. Fucking watch your mouth!

PINA

Nino, tell me it's not true.

NINO

It's not ... true.

ANGELO

(*shocked*) What?

NINO

Angelo ... I never really was ...

ANGELO

You never really were what?

NINO

You know.

ANGELO

Gay?

NINO

Yeah.

LINA

Phase. Told you. *Andiamo.*

ANGELO

That's bullshit. You're just as gay as I am!

PINA

I'm gonna be sick.

NINO

(*to PINA*) Don't listen to him.

ANGELO

You're playing it straight just 'cause your *mammina*'s here.

NINO

Look Angelo I don't … This is not what I want anymore, okay? You're just gonna have to deal with it.

ANGELO

What don't you want? Me? Us?

NINO

I'm sorry I was going through a …

ANGELO

(*livid*) If you say a phase I swear I'm gonna kill you! (*a beat, more relaxed*) Nino come on. I don't know what happened between you and … but don't do this okay? (*starting to sink in, search for words*) Don't do this … Let's … Let's just go home, okay?

> ANGELO *tries to grab Nino's hand. NINO pushes him away.*

Nino come on, you can't be serious, Nino …

NINO

Just back off!

ANGELO

(*baffled*) What is this about? My God! What's going on?

MARIA

Leave him be, Angelo.

ANGELO

Leave him be? Ma, this isn't some kid who doesn't wanna play with me anymore, this is my …

NINO

(*angry, does not want to hear the word, "lover"*) Shut your fucking mouth! I said I don't want this anymore. *No more*! Understood, Angelo? *Basta*!

> *ANGELO shakes his head. Nothing makes sense. He covers his face with his hands.*

MARIA

Don't be upset.

ANGELO

Don't be upset, ma? How can I not? My whole life is crashing around me, and you don't want me to be upset? ... Were you in on this? Were you in on this?

MARIA

You know you're welcome to move back with us anytime.

ANGELO

(*sarcastic*) Oh! What a comfort! (*serious*) I've done my time, ma. So you can forget about it.

MARIA

Time? What time?

ANGELO

I served almost thirty years in this prison. ... This prison of guilt, of fear, of lies and of abuse, I'm not about to come back.

MARIA

(*adamant*) We have never abused you!

ANGELO

Oh no? Instilling the fear of anything and anyone who wasn't Italian, what do you call that? The epic guilt trips, your endless trials and tribulations ... We couldn't even cross the street without calling to tell you we had made it to the other side safely.

MARIA

You would have liked it better to have a key hanging around your neck? To have no one to feed you a hot meal when you came home from school? Like those other kids whose mothers abandoned them to go to work?

ANGELO

No, no, no. Not tonight. Don't pull an Italian *mamma* thing tonight because my pain is much stronger and much fiercer than anything you can come up with.

MARIA

Had you listened to your father and me.

ANGELO

I would have what? Married some good Italian girl and pretended I had feelings for her? You would have preferred that? Why am I asking? Of course you would have. Because the outside world would think I was straight, and my happiness is much less important than what other people think!

NINO

Angelo, we heard enough.

ANGELO

Take a good look Nino. This is gonna be you in twenty years.

MARIA

You sacrifice your life for your children only to hear that all along they were miserable.

ANGELO

Miserable. That's right. Miserable like you can't even imagine. Going to school everyday being called fag this

and fag that by stupid bimbos like the one you invited
here tonight ...

PINA

Hey!

ANGELO

Waking up every morning hoping that I would get
through the day without being humiliated ... I spent
the formative years of my life feeling like a piece of
shit, ma. Feeling *ashamed.* Trying desperately to fit in,
but my *paesani* they never let me in because I was a fag.
And you know what they do to fags in Italian high
schools, ma? Do you? They kill them! Not physically,
but mentally they destroy them by chipping away at
their dignity day after day after day, 'til you don't care
anymore. 'Til you're so numb that all you wanna do is
disappear. Go somewhere where no one is ever gonna
bother you again. But there is no such place ma. There
is no such refuge.

MARIA

(*upset*) Why didn't you ever say anything?

> *GINO starts to rub his stomach:*

GINO

Owwww!

ANNA

Angelo I think that's enough.

ANGELO

That's right. Pa is rubbing his stomach. I wouldn't
wanna trigger one of his psychosomatic attacks.

GINO

I wouldn't wish this pain on my worst enemy.

ANGELO

(*applauding*) Bravo! Bravo! The Italian martyr bit.
Better to suffer like Jesus on the cross than inflict pain
on your worst enemy or your children!

(*to NINO*) Are you still paying close attention Nino,
'cause this is gonna be your life!

MARIA

What's wrong with our lives!

ANGELO

Where would you like me to start? I mean, the only
worthwhile thing you ever did was leave that spit of a
village of yours in Italy to come here. And hadn't it
been for the war that forced you out, you would still be
there, wouldn't you?

LINA

You better believe it!

ANGELO

But you never really left. 'Cause when you came here,
you brought that little spit of a village along and
dropped it on this country, in your houses like a big
pile of bricks. And we were forced to live there too. In
1950s Italy. With all the gossip, and the jealousy, and
the lies.

MARIA

(*on the brink of tears*) You're the one who lied to us, not
the other way around.

ANGELO

I lied to you because, that's what you wanted, ma.
That's how you raised me.

MARIA

I did not raise you to be a liar!

ANGELO
How did Aunt Yolanda die?

MARIA tries to answer then begins to cry.

What's funny to me is that, even after coming all this way, you didn't even bother to do anything constructive with yourselves. You chose to spend, what is it now? Thirty, forty years, reminiscing about your little, worthless, lives in that spit of a village.

LINA
Listen you, our lives are not worthless.

ANGELO
Worthless! All your lives are completely worthless … Cry ma, cry … Unlike Pa I want to inflict my pain. On all of you. Because it's stronger than my guilt right now. So cry. Cry over your ingrate son. Your dead sister. Or your stupid, worthless life!

ANNA goes up to ANGELO and slaps him in the face.

And there we have it. The slap! The end to the quintessential Italian melodrama. The long-suffering sister. The thankless son. The martyr mother. The baffled lover, his stupid mistress. And the smack in the face! It's been a lovely evening, but I must go. I hope you all have a good time in your respective cocoons. If anyone wants to get in touch with me … I'll be living in the real world.

ANGELO is about to exit, he stops in front of PINA.

But first, there's something I have to do.

ANGELO pulls on Pina's hair.

PINA
Owwwww!

ANGELO

God help us, it's real!

ANGELO leaves.

Blackout. End of Act One.

ACT TWO

Scene 1: Nino's Office

Special goes up on NINO, who is dressed in a suit and tie. He sits at his desk, buried in paperwork. He looks up and talks to the audience.

NINO

I lost my father when I was seventeen. And if I sit quietly long enough, I can still hear my mother screaming. Screaming her pain out loud.

(*goes back to work, beat, addresses audience*) About three months before my high school graduation, they found something on my father's lungs. A spot, my mother said. We had planned our summer vacation for right after I finished school that summer to celebrate my graduation: his only child had made it through high school and was going off to college to become somebody ...

(*goes back to work, beat, addresses audience*) When my father came here from Italy, he got a job washing windows for 75 cents an hour. So he had to spend his days looking inside office towers at people being somebodies, while he was outside being no one. Scrubbing the dirt and grime so that the somebodies could be seen better.

(*goes back to work, beat, addresses audience*) Turns out the "spot" was cancer. And it spread so quickly that within a month my father was not my father anymore. He wasn't the healthy, powerful man that had raised me. Within a month the cancer had carried him away and in his place was a powerless, frightened being who barely had the strength to speak. But speak he did ... "Take care of your mother," he'd say. "Go to school, get married, and dance at your grandkids' wedding for me."

(*goes back to work, beat, addresses the audience*) We never sent him to a hospital. Nor hired a private nurse. Not even in the final days. Me and my mom took care of him. Bathed him, shaved him, fed him. Gave him all the pills that made him sicker than he already was. I thought that if he took his medicine he'd get better, but ...

(*goes back to work, beat, addresses audience*) So graduation time came along. I didn't wanna go, but he insisted. When I got home, I showed him my diploma. And for a breath of a moment he became the healthy, powerful man that had raised me. For a breath of a moment he was my father again. A breath that seemed like an eternity for me and my mom. But that was only a breath to him.

(*goes back to work, beat, addresses audience*) He died that summer.

(*beat*) So here I am. Being somebody in an office tower. The windows are sparkling. But there's no one here to see me.

> *Crossfade to:*

Scene 2: Gino and Maria's House

GINO is sitting on the couch. MARIA comes in, distraught, holding an invitation to Nino's wedding in her hand.

MARIA

"*Disgraziata!*" That woman's a "*disgraziata!*"

GINO

What now?

MARIA

Listen to this!

(*reading from the invitation*) *La Signora* Lina Paventi is honoured to invite you to the wedding of her son Nino … do I have to go on?

GINO

Nino's getting married?

MARIA

To Pina.

GINO has no clue who PINA is.

La putana.

Now he knows.

And look at this, she even includes a handwritten note: Dear Maria & Gino: I'm sorry for what happened. Please see this invitation as a peace offering. I pray San Giuseppe you can make it. Love, Lina.

GINO

What's wrong with that?

MARIA

You gotta read between the lines. What this really says is: Dear Maria & Gino: I'm sorry your son is still an *omosessuale.* Please see this invitation as proof that mine is not. I pray San Giuseppe you can make it, so you can watch me gloat. Love, Lina.

GINO

Disgraziata! Tear up the invitation!

MARIA

No! I'm gonna send it back. R.S.V.P.: "*Va fa 'nculo,* you and your entire *famiglia!*" Love, Maria and Gino! ... And we're not sending them a gift!

GINO

No gift!

MARIA

Ma sei matto? We gotta get them a gift. You want Lina to think we're cheap?

GINO

Nobody thinks I'm cheap. We'll make out a check for two hundred dollars, and then we won't show up!

MARIA

Ma sei scemo? We can't not show up ... she's gonna tell everyone that we're jealous.

GINO

Jealous? Jealous of what? We're going! But I'm not buying a new suit.

MARIA

Now you want look like a bum?

GINO

We'll go shopping tomorrow! The best suit, the most beautiful dress, and the biggest gift. That'll show her!

MARIA

Yeah! We'll go, but we'll have a lousy time.

GINO

We'll look at our watches, and yawn all night long.

MARIA

We can't have a lousy time. Then she's gonna think we're angry.

GINO

We'll dance 'til dawn, just to spite her!

MARIA

If we dance 'til dawn then she's gonna think we're putting up a good front!

GINO

We'll ... We'll ... (*exhausted*) Mari, this is making me tired.

MARIA

I can't believe he's getting married. So soon!

GINO

Do you think they invited Angelo?

MARIA

Angelo wants nothing to do with us, didn't he make that clear? And after what he said to me, I want nothing to do with him! I don't even wanna know if he's alive or dead!

GINO

Where's Anna?

MARIA

Spending the night at Angelo's.

GINO

Then we'll know in the morning if he's okay?

MARIA

We'll know in the morning.

    Crossfade to:

Scene 3: Angelo's Apartment

ANGELO is working on his laptop, ANNA enters, suitcases in hand. ANGELO does not see her. She approaches to take a closer look at what he's writing. He turns around. He screams. She screams. They both scream together.

ANGELO

Are you trying to gimme a heart attack?

ANNA

You're the one who scared me with your screaming!

ANGELO

It's a normal reaction when there's an intruder in your apartment.

ANNA

(*insulted*) Since when is your sister an intruder?

ANGELO

What's with the suitcases?

ANNA

I'm moving out.

ANNA plops herself on the sofa.

ANGELO

And the problem with this apartment is?

ANNA

Nothing! Why does there have to be a problem?

ANGELO

The bad luck has worn off?

ANNA

Yes! Oh Angelo I can't wait for you to see this place. It's the apartment of my dreams!

ANGELO
Well congratulations!

ANNA
(*looks through her purse*) Thanks! I'm outta of cigarettes. Do you have anything?

ANGELO
Do *I* have anything. Hold on.

> ANGELO *rummages through the drawers of his entertainment centre (television stand/VCR/library/bar.) He takes out a bag, then a bottle of whiskey.*

(*setting everything, along with a pack of cigarettes on the coffee table*) You see, the great thing about losing the love of your life and becoming depressed, is that you're able to sucker your doctor into getting you a prescription for anything.

ANNA
(*excited*) Fiorinals! You even got Fiorinals!

> ANNA *immediately pops one.*

ANGELO
Remember when we used to steal these from ma?

ANNA
Yeah, she'd take them for her killer migraines.

ANGELO
Only we took more than her.

ANNA
She was always rushing to the pharmacy.

(*imitates MARIA*) "I don't understand I just had this prescription filled, Gino what's going on?"

ANGELO
(*imitates GINO*) "You're a junky that's what's going on."

ANNA

(*imitates MARIA*) "I'm a junky? I'm a junky!"

Both laugh. ANGELO pops a Fiorinal. Beat.

ANGELO

How did our parents take it?

ANNA

Take what?

ANGELO

Your moving out.

ANNA

I don't know.

ANGELO

You didn't tell them?

ANNA

No.

ANGELO

But they're gonna be sick with worry … at least call to say that you're spending the night here.

ANNA

(*irritated*) Can you please let me handle this my way?

ANGELO

I'm sorry. You're right. Who am I? Look at the mess I made of everything.

ANNA

You know, sometimes I wonder how all this happened. I mean, we were happy kids, weren't we? Life was pretty much all figured out for us and then bam! Everything gets all twisted. You're estranged from everybody and I'm running away from home.

ANGELO starts to laugh. A giddy mood prevails throughout the scene (unless otherwise indicated) because of the drugs.

ANNA
What is so funny?

ANGELO
Running away from home? Anna, you're almost forty.

ANNA
Hey, we're Italian ... I could be eighty and it would still be considered running away.

ANGELO laughs harder. ANNA chuckles.

Stop it.

ANGELO
We are so *messed up.*

ANNA
Yeah.

ANGELO
Do you realize how messed up we are?

ANNA
Yeah. Hand me another Fiorinal.

ANGELO gives ANNA another pill, he pops one too.

ANGELO
I envy you, you know.

ANNA
That's a first.

ANGELO
Starting a new life. I remember how exciting it was when I first moved out ...

(*suggesting boredom, disappointment*) But now …

(*frustrated*) Damn! I wanna get out of this city so bad.

ANNA

Oh no! To go where?

ANGELO

L.A., New York, I dunno. I'm sick of it here nothing moves— especially in what I do. I mean, does L.A. give a shit that I write sitcoms in Montreal? And New York— they don't give a damn about my plays …

ANNA

So go!

ANGELO

But Montreal, man. That cross on the mountain; it's like a magnet. No matter how far you get away it always … (*gets in a crucified position*) pulls you back. I'm wasting my life!

ANNA

Okay … I think now would be a good time to name five things we are grateful for.

ANGELO

(*put off*) Oh please, Anna, nooo …

ANNA

Ah come on. Come on … I'll go first. I'm grateful for my wonderful brother Angelo and … Fiorinal and— (*discouraged, she can't find a third*) Your turn.

ANGELO

I'm grateful for, (*as if forced to say it*) my wonderful sister Anna.

ANNA

Grazie!

ANGELO
And … Fiorinal.

ANNA
No that's mine!

ANGELO
Okay, then I'm grateful for … Oh, I know …
(*snickering*) Gay saunas!

ANNA
What are those like?

ANGELO
No, no, no. You're too young.

ANNA
(*like a little girl*) Please! Please! I wanna know! I wanna
know! I wanna know *everything*!

ANGELO
Well, you go in. Rent either a room or a locker. Take
your clothes off, put on a towel, cruise around, pick a
partner and dosy-doh!

ANNA
(*disappointed*) Just like that? And then what?

ANGELO
(*pensive*) Then you go home. You swear to yourself
you'll never go back … But somehow you always find
yourself back there, walking around like a zombie.
Searching, waiting in the dark. Thinking that the next
experience will be better than the previous, but it
never is.

> *Beat. ANNA consoles her brother then:*

ANNA
(*looks at her watch*) Shit! I gotta go.

> *ANNA gets up, woozy from the Fiorinal.*

ANGELO
I'll drive you.

ANNA
You're in no state to drive.

> ANNA *opens her purse, dumps the cigarettes, and all the pill bottles in. ANGELO stops her when she is about to take off with the whiskey.*

ANNA
I'll take a cab.

ANGELO
So this is it, huh? My big sister's moving out.

ANNA
(*frightened*) No.

ANGELO
Whaddya mean, no?

ANNA
I can't Angelo, I thought I could but I can't!

ANGELO
(*compassionate*) Anna if you don't go tonight, you'll never …

ANNA
And I'll deal with it! Just call me a cab!

ANGELO
But Anna—

ANNA
Do I have to do it myself?

> ANNA *sullenly picks up her suitcases. Crossfade to:*

Scene 4: Street (Plaza St. Hubert)

PINA and LINA enter walking arm in arm.

PINA

Che bella giornata ... I hope it's gonna be this beautiful on my wedding day.

LINA

Don't worry. I said a novena, and all the neighborhood will be hanging their rosary beads on the clotheslines the night before.

PINA

What for?

LINA

So it doesn't rain on your wedding day. Didn't your *mamma* teach you nothing? (*notices someone in the distance, to PINA*) Cross the street! Cross the street! Cross the street!

PINA

Wha? What?

LINA

Too late ... just smile and shut your mouth!

> *MARIA and GINO enter from the opposite side of the stage, carrying shopping bags.*

(*all smiles*) Gino ... Maria! What are you two doing here, huh?

MARIA

(*a little cold*) A little shopping. *Come stai*, Lina?

LINA

Bene, bene. You remember the blushing bride?

GINO

She may be a bride but it's been a long time since *she's* blushed!

All laugh a polite laugh.

LINA

Always with the sick jokes. This guy kills me. Pina, say hi.

PINA

Hi.

MARIA

So, the big day is gonna be here soon.

LINA

Oh! I got your R.S.V.P. Maria, I can't tell you how happy I was to see that you were gonna be there. I got down on my knees and thanked San Francesco, 'cause I had been praying to him that you'd let bygones be bygones, and come to this blessed event.

MARIA

You wrote me you were praying to San Giuseppe.

LINA

San Giuseppe was taking some time off!

> *LINA laughs at her own joke. The rest laugh along. Quietly.*

Wait 'til you see her wedding dress, Maria. When she first put it on, I cried like a baby. She looks like the Madonna.

MARIA

I'm sure the Madonna is real happy about that. We have to get going, we'll see you at the wedding, ah? *Ciao!*

*MARIA and GINO go on their way when LINA stops
them by saying:*

LINA

Let me just take a minute here to tell you that I'm so
sorry for what happened at your house that night.

MARIA

Mah, there's nothing to be sorry about.

LINA

And I think what Angelo said to you was disgusting!

GINO

He was upset.

MARIA

Yeah, he was upset.

LINA

Now he's alone like a dog, and that's what he deserves.

MARIA

Who says he's alone like a dog?

GINO

Yeah. Who says?

LINA

Why? You speak to him? I just assumed ...

MARIA

It's always a mistake to assume.

GINO

Big mistake to assume.

LINA

He moved back in with you?

MARIA

Why would he wanna do that? He's an adult!

GINO

Adults should live on their own!

LINA

Whatever you say … I just pray he'll find himself a nice Italian girl.

MARIA

He won't find himself a nice Italian girl. *He's gay!*

GINO

(*proudly*) No one's gayer than my son!

MARIA

(*gloating*) And he's got a new boyfriend!

GINO

A gorgeous man!

MARIA

Loves Angelo to death!

GINO

I should love my wife, like this guy loves Angelo!

LINA

So … everything turned out for the best.

MARIA

Things couldn't be better!

LINA

Good! Pina, come on *bella*. We're gonna be late. (*to MARIA and GINO*) *Ciao*, ah!

PINA

Ciao!

MARIA

(*waving*) *Arrivederci!*

GINO
(*waving, under his breath*) *Pozza n'accire!* [Translation: May someone kill you!]

> *LINA shoots him a dirty look. Smiling:*

MARIA & GINO
Ciao!

LINA
Pozza n'accire!

> *MARIA and GINO shoot a dirty look.*

LINA & PINA
Ciao!

> *LINA and PINA exit. MARIA frowns at her husband:*

MARIA
No one's gayer than my son?

> *GINO shrugs his shoulders. MARIA and GINO look at each other, then burst out laughing.*

You're gonna kill me, you!

> *The two laugh as lights crossfade to:*

Scene 5: Angelo's Apartment

> *NINO enters, slowly. Looks around. Sits on the couch. ANGELO enters. He sees NINO. ANGELO doesn't know how to react.*

NINO
I never gave you back my set of keys. So today I figured I should give you my keys back.

> *NINO tosses the keys on the coffee table.*

NINO

I should have called, but it was a spur-of-the-moment thing.

ANGELO

I'd forgotten you had them.

NINO

Me too. Then I was going through my pockets, and there they were.

ANGELO

Funny how we always find things when we're not looking for them.

NINO

Yeah ... funny.

ANGELO

You don't have to go right away.

NINO

I wasn't. How you been, Angelo?

ANGELO

How do you think?

NINO

Believe me Angelo, what happened ... it was for the best.

ANGELO

It was?

NINO

No listen. This marriage thing ... it's really cool.

ANGELO

Nino, please don't try to convert me.

NINO

I'm not, but listen, you should give it a try. I know
you're seeing a new guy but—

ANGELO

(*surprised*) A new guy?

NINO

Yeah. Your mom told my mom the other day. Says your
parents were acting as though being a homosexual was
normal.

ANGELO

(*in disbelief*) My mother said that I was seeing *a man*?

NINO

Yeah, and that's great but listen … you should really
give this thing a shot, man. Find yourself a nice Italian
girl. Maybe I could hook you up.

ANGELO

Nino what are you talking about?

NINO

I never meant to hurt you.

ANGELO

Well you did a pretty good job.

NINO

I'm sorry you had to learn about me and Pina the way
you did but—

ANGELO

Did you ever love me?

NINO

Aw come on. That's not fair.

ANGELO

Did you?

Beat.

NINO
We had a very special friendship.

Not what ANGELO wanted to hear.

ANGELO
I loved you.

NINO
Angelo …

ANGELO
I still love you.

NINO
(*softly*) I'm not the right guy to love … we had a thing together and it was fun, but now it's over. You have a new friend. I have a new life. You'll see, everything's gonna be alright. Huh, Angelo? Tell me you're gonna be alright.

ANGELO
Are you gonna be alright? The straight life, it's what you really want?

The two look at each other. Their eyes lock. For a moment the audience must believe that they are about to make up. NINO slowly, gently caresses Angelo's face. ANGELO closes his eyes: so good to feel the familiar touch of his ex. Beat. NINO pulls away and leaves the apartment before he changes his mind. Lights fade as:

(*poetic, emotional*) Everything goes dark, except for Nino. Now Nino is gone … And all I can see … Is just how dark … darkness can be.

Blackout.

Scene 6: Cemetery

Light comes up on MARIA and GINO at the cemetery. They are sitting on a bench. MARIA sullenly looks at her sister's grave as GINO sleeps. MARIA noticing her husband sleeping:

MARIA

Gino!

(*louder*) Gino!

(*loudest*) Gino!

    GINO wakes up.

GINO

I wasn't sleeping.

MARIA

Do you have to fall asleep every time we visit my sister?

GINO

What does she care? She's dead!

MARIA

Don't be rude!

    A beat.

GINO

Maria, let's go home. I'm tired.

MARIA

In a minute ... I'm thinking of getting her a statue. Do you think she'd like that? A statue?

GINO

A statue of who?

MARIA

Santa Yolanda, like her name.

GINO
There is no Santa Yolanda.

MARIA
Who says?

GINO
I say!

MARIA
(*shouting*) You wouldn't know!

GINO
(*shouting*) Why wouldn't I know?

MARIA
(*shouting*) 'Cause you know nothing!

GINO
(*shouting*) I know nothing? *I* know nothing?

MARIA
(*shouting*) Yeah! You know nothing!

    A beat.

GINO
(*sullen, serious*) Everyday Maria ... Everyday I pray that I go to my grave before you, because you're right ... I know nothing.

MARIA
What are you saying? You know plenty!

GINO
When Angelo left us ... it scared me Mari, it made me think of what would happen if you left me ... Nothing in this world makes sense to me, except you ... so please, don't go before me ...

MARIA
No one's going anywhere.

GINO

I couldn't stand it. Not waking up next to your beautiful face. I just couldn't take it.

MARIA

Gino, my face hasn't been beautiful since the fifties.

GINO

(*lovingly*) What do you know?

MARIA

(*lovingly*) I know, Gi. I know.

> *GINO gently caresses Maria's face. The two kiss. Beat. MARIA stares at her sister's grave.*

(*sighs heavily*) Angelo and Yolanda. One of a kind.

GINO

How do you mean?

MARIA

She was different too, you know.

GINO

She was a *omosessuale*?

MARIA

Who knows? ... But she always had it in her head that she wanted to be different. She wanted to go to New York and act on Broadway, or, to Hollywood to become the next Marilyn Monroe. Never had the intention of settling down. But we forced her. Me and my mother. We found her a good man. Married her. And she was miserable. So miserable! Her too, she thought our lives were worthless. All the time she would say: Maria, you're worthless.

GINO

Worthless?

MARIA

Worthless. Why do you think I cried so much when
Angelo said that? It's as if Yolanda came back to haunt
me. I realized that all the mistakes I had made with my
baby sister, I had repeated them with my son … We
were all so afraid for her. Scared that if she lived this
life she had in her head, she would've ended up in a
bad way. And look where she ended up. At 33.

(*crying*) Bunch of idiots we were. Kept on feeding her
pills to calm her down, instead of letting her fly. Then
one day she flew. Straight into the river. What a way of
giving us all the finger!

GINO

Mari, that was an accident.

MARIA

It was no accident, Gi. No accident. Come on, it's time
to go. *Andiamo.*

> *GINO and MARIA get up. Beat.*

GINO

(*to grave*) Take care, Yolanda!

MARIA

(*sullenly,t o grave*) Take care.

> *GINO and MARIA exit. Crossfade to:*

Scene 7: Angelo's Apartment

*Very depressing music plays. Lights are dim. ANNA and
ANGELO sit on the couch smoking cigarettes. ANGELO is
at his lowest. ANNA seems to be enjoying the song, then
disenchanted:*

ANNA

Where the *hell* do you get this music?

ANGELO does not respond.

You gonna spend the rest of your life moping around?

Exasperated, ANNA grabs the CD player's remote control and shuts the music off. Then getting up to turn up the lights:

Okay; I think the time has come for me to take matters into hand.

ANGELO

You can't even get your own life straight, now you wanna mess up mine?

ANNA

I'm bad with my own life, but I'm good with others and I'm telling you Angelo you're gonna get cancer if you continue this way!

ANGELO

Gee thanks.

ANNA

So things got a little out of hand, but look at you now! You're *gay*! Isn't that great! You even have a village! Do I have a village? No!

ANGELO looks at ANNA as if she were crazy.

I mean ... you can even ... um ... (*enlightening moment*) march ... at gay pride!

ANGELO

(*not impressed*) Gay pride?

ANNA

(*cheerful*) I'll come with you! (*angry*) I'm trying to be helpful here can you perhaps show a shred of enthusiasm?

ANGELO

No.

ANNA

(*pleading*) Come on Angelo, do it for me. I feel soooo guilty!

ANGELO

Why?

ANNA

Because. I'm the one who suggested you—

ANGELO

(*cutting her off*) Come out. Yes! And look at the mess you put me in!

ANNA

(*insulted*) What are you talking about? I didn't put you in this mess!

ANGELO

With your: "studies prove this and studies prove that!"

ANNA

So you were comfortable living a lie?

ANGELO

Yes! Now can you please go before you cause anymore damage!

ANNA

Gladly!

> *She grabs the remote control, is about to turn the music back on when, emotional:*

Angelo … Don't turn into me. One stuck sibling in the family is enough.

This hits home for ANGELO, but he denies it.

ANGELO

I'm nothing like you.

ANNA

(*angry*) Ooooh! I should tear my tongue out the next time I try to help you!

ANNA is about to storm off when ANGELO stops her with:

ANGELO

Okay I'm stuck, happy? I came out of the closet because I felt stuck. And now I feel even more stuck. I mean I lost my family, I lost my lover.

ANNA

Angelo, if you wanted nothing to change, why did you bother to come out?

ANGELO

Because you made me!

ANNA, angry, knowing he's bullshitting her:

ANNA

Right! Like *I've* always been a *big* influence in your life!

ANNA is about to exit when ANGELO:

ANGELO

(*quickly*) Because I didn't want our parents to die not knowing who I really was.

Beat. Both ANGELO and ANNA become teary-eyed.

Our parents deserve to know their son … not an illusion or a delusion of who I am … but who I am for real … it's the least I could do for them … out of

respect ... out of love ... the least I could do ... I did it
all wrong ... and maybe ... it was wrong of me to do it
but ...

> *ANNA rushes into her brother's arms. Both cry. Beat.*

ANNA
> (*proudly*) Damn! I'm good!

>> *Both ANGELO and ANNA laugh and cry as lights fade
>> to black.*

Scene 8: Confession Booth

> *Wash fades in on confession booth. ANGELO sits in the
> "priest's" compartment, ANNA kneels in one of the
> booths. MARIA enters, kneels crosses herself and:*

MARIA
> *Perdonami padre,* for I have sinned.

> *No response.*

> (*louder*) *Perdonami padre,* for I have sinned.

> (*knocking on the booth*) Is anyone in there?

> *ANGELO opens the little curtain.*

ANGELO
> (*clears his throat*) Yes?

MARIA
> Twice I have taken the name of the Lord ...

ANGELO
> Ma, it's me!

MARIA
> (*beat*) Angelo?

ANGELO
Yes.

MARIA
Are you crazy! What are you doing in there?

ANGELO
We have to talk, ma.

MARIA
At confession?

ANGELO
Forgive me mother for I have sinned.

MARIA
Ah shuddup!

ANGELO
I have called you and your life worthless and for that, I am truly sorry.

MARIA
Oh yeah? Why now?

ANGELO
Whaddya mean, why now?

MARIA
I mean why did you wait all this time to be sorry? You realize the pain you put me through?

ANNA
Cut him some slack.

MARIA
(*looks up*) Who's that?

ANNA
The holy spirit, *mamma.*

MARIA
Anna, where are you?

ANNA
 In the other booth.

MARIA
 What have you two done to Padre Carmignani?

ANGELO & ANNA
 We bribed him.

ANNA
 With a bottle of wine and a carton of cigarettes.

 GINO enters Maria's "booth."

GINO
 Mari, what's taking you so long?

MARIA
 Will you get outta here? I'm trying to confess myself.

GINO
 You have sins?

MARIA
 Yes! I have sins!

GINO
 (*to "priest"*) Padre, she won't let me touch her anymore, isn't that a mortal sin?

MARIA
 Will you stop! Angelo's in there.

GINO
 Our Angelo?

ANGELO
 How are you Pa?

GINO
 Hey Angelo! You became a priest?

MARIA

Worse! He bribed Father Carmignani! A bottle of wine and a carton of cigarettes. Can you believe that?

GINO

No! (*beat*) He usually settles for a bottle of wine. Angelo you got screwed!

ANNA

You guys bribed him already?

MARIA

Only once.

GINO

To bump up the date of Angelo's first communion so I could put my mother on the first boat back to Italy. She wouldn't leave until she saw her grandson swallow the body of Christ for the first time. Like that she could die in peace—and she's still around—who am I talking to?

MARIA

Your daughter.

GINO

Anna, did you see my "Forza Italia" hat? Your mother lost it again.

MARIA

Would you please … Our son is trying to apologize to us.

GINO

Angelo, just forget that night ever happened.

ANNA

We can't forget it happened because then it'll just happen again.

ANGELO

You know Ma, I realize that what I said to you was awful, but what you did, trying to set me up with Pina and stuff, that was pretty low.

GINO

I told her it was a stupid idea.

MARIA

Aw shuddup! ... Besides, it was Lina's idea.

ANNA

Will you guys stop putting the blame on everyone but yourselves?

MARIA & GINO

We will if you will.

ANGELO & ANNA

We don't do that.

MARIA

Only since you were kids. Whenever something went wrong it was always our fault or Italy's fault. I know we weren't the perfect parents and we don't come from the perfect country, but we did do some things right.

ANGELO

Some things.

MARIA

And we are not worthless! *Hai capito?*

ANGELO

I apologized for that already.

MARIA

Well let me tell you, you haven't finished!

ANGELO

What about the apology you owe me?

MARIA

Come to supper tonight, if you're willing to step back in that prison …

ANGELO

I'm sorry about that too.

MARIA

Come to supper, and we'll see.

ANGELO

Can I bring my new boyfriend?

MARIA

What new boyfriend?

ANGELO

The one you told Lina about.

ANNA

What!?!

ANGELO

(*to ANNA*) Can you believe? They told her I had a new boyfriend and that I was madly in love.

> *ANNA laughs.*

MARIA

I guess we're not all tragedy, guilt and fear, after all.

> *They all laugh. ANNA blurts out:*

ANNA

I'm moving out!

MARIA, GINO, ANGELO

What?!?

ANNA

I'm moving out. I'm leaving home. I love you guys very much, but it's something I just have to do—I'm sorry.

Beat.

MARIA

It's about time! *Andiamo!*

GINO

How are we gonna get outta here?

ANNA

If anyone sees us coming out at the same time, they'll talk.

ANGELO

I'm sure they're already talking because of your fag son, right ma?

MARIA

Please Angelo, they been talking since my sister died.

GINO

I say we all come out together.

MARIA

All together with our heads high up in the sky! But before we do ... kids ... I have something to tell you.

ANGELO

What ma?

MARIA

(*sullen, serious*) Your Aunt Yolanda ... Her death was no accident. She committed suicide. And it's time that you knew.

A beat.

ANNA & ANGELO

We knew.

MARIA

Whaddya mean, you knew?

All step out of the confessional together.

ANNA

It doesn't take a rocket scientist to figure it out, ma.

MARIA

Why didn't you ever say anything?

ANGELO

You always became hysterical when we mentioned her name.

MARIA

I been carrying this secret in my heart for all these years and all along you knew!

(*to audience*) They knew!

ANGELO

(*exiting*) Don't make a federal case outta this.

MARIA

(*exiting*) I don't need *you* to tell *me* if I can make a federal case outta this!

ANNA

(*exiting to MARIA*) Do we have to pass by the grocery store before we go home?

MARIA

(*offstage*) Yeah, we're outta cheese.

GINO

(*beaming, looks up*) Hey boss! Thanks for giving me my *famiglia* back, ah!

> *GINO exits. Wash crossfades to:*

Scene 9: Angelo's Apartment

Crowds are heard cheering in the distance. Background dance music is also heard. It is gay pride day. ANGELO is watching from his window. ANNA enters.

ANNA
    You look great.

ANGELO
    (*not believing her*) Sure I do.

> *ANNA takes ANGELO by the hand. Brings him center-stage. Wash fades to black except for special on ANGELO and ANNA. ANNA gently turns ANGELO to face stage right.*

ANNA
    Don't take my word for it. Look at yourself in the mirror ...

> *Special comes up on NINO (wearing tuxedo pants and a dress shirt with a bow tie) and PINA (in a smashing wedding dress) facing ANNA and ANGELO. They are exactly in the same position, ANGELO and NINO being each other's "mirror." ANGELO and NINO never take their eyes off their "reflections."*

    Not bad huh?

NINO
    No. Not bad at all.

> *PINA helps NINO put a vest on, while ANNA helps ANGELO put a vest on. Throughout the mirror sequence, all of Angelo's and Nino's moves are a reflection of each other.*

ANNA
    How you feeling?

NINO
    Scared.

PINA

It's normal to be scared.

> *PINA helps NINO put his tuxedo jacket on. ANNA helps ANGELO put his jean jacket on.*

ANGELO

Am I really gonna be happier now?

PINA

I dunno. But at least—

ANNA

You're on your way.

> *NINO turns to PINA. ANGELO turns to ANNA. PINA puts a carnation in Nino's lapel. ANNA sticks an Aids ribbon on ANGELO. They turn ANGELO and NINO to face the audience. PINA and ANNA are behind them.*

PINA & ANNA

On your way!

> *NINO takes PINA by the hand, they go upstage and dance. Special tightens on ANGELO. (He is now alone on stage) ANGELO is at gay pride. Crowd noises and dance music can be heard. A quarter way through Angelo's speech, (indicated by *) the special fades on NINO and PINA. They kiss as special fades.*

ANGELO

So I was on my way. At gay pride. On that day. As the crowds around me cheered, I was on my way. To where. I didn't know. To what. I didn't care. But I was there. With sluggish steps and sheepish waves. I was there. Not knowing where I was going. But acknowledging where I had been … I was my present that day, but I was also my past. All the voices, all the memories, all the victories, all the defeats. Marching with me that day, all the pieces that had been hidden and all that had been revealed. I was whole that day as the crowds cheered me, somehow I was whole(*) … I was the sun-kissed piazzas, and I was Stonewall. I was the drag queens, and I was the mountaintop villages, clinging for dear life as their age had rendered them too frail to withstand even the slightest gust of wind, and yet they stood, after centuries of wind *we* stood, and marched and shouted and waved that day. I was Italiano, proud, and gay … And as each step became smoother, and every wave, a song, I realized that for the first time, there was no shame, on that day. For the first time. *I was not ashamed! …*

> *As ANGELO speaks, a MAN appears on stage. The lights are dim, so we cannot tell who he is. The MAN is sitting on a bench, draped in a towel.*

I wished Nino could be there. Proud and not ashamed with me there. But would he have been? My beloved on that day, could he have been?

> *It is revealed that the MAN in question is NINO sitting in a gay sauna. Waiting. (NOTE: It must be very clear that he is in a gay sauna.) Light goes out on NINO.*

But then I thought of my Aunt Yolanda, on my way, my sweet Aunt Yolanda, on that day, and remembered that, when everyone was still dancing the Tarantella, she died, trying to teach them how to Mambo.

> *Upbeat dance music plays, ANGELO dances. He is smiling, ecstatic, as he dances. He turns his back to the audience, while still dancing, and dances his way upstage. Dances off into the horizon. Dances towards his new life.*

The End.